King Nebuchadnezzar

Words and Music © 1998 Teresa Skinner
Illustrations © 2004 JAWA Art Publisher
All Rights Reserved
Teresa Skinner – JAWA Art Publisher
PO Box 26632 Prescott Valley, AZ 86312
www.teresaskinner.com
jawa-art@as.net

This book is dedicated to Daniel and Moises.
You've kept our world active and filled it with joy.

Special Acknowledgements:

Many thanks to all of the Artists for your great work:

George Thomas
Annella Whitehead
Kimberly Etter
Sue Wood
Teresa Skinner

Special recognition to Erica Caceres and Cindy Richhart
for your artistic contributions.

Special thanks to Agnes I. Numer for showing us how to get here.

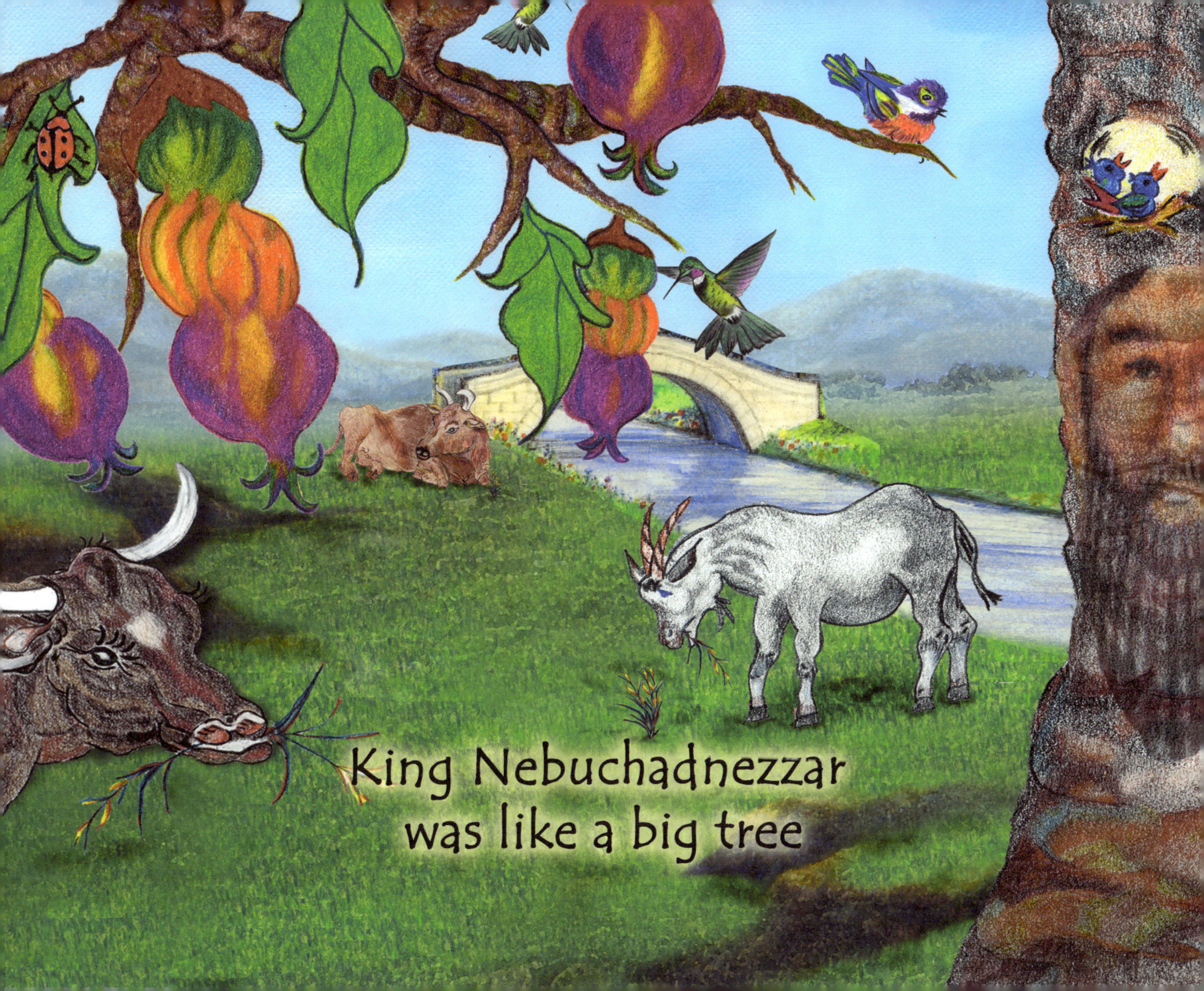

Growing hair from the dew

Then one day that tree did fall

It was a lesson shown to all.

Growing hair from the dew

But then one day the king came to,
the mind and throne that he once knew.

You know this king then had a son.

King Belshazzar he was the one.

Came a Hand to the wall...

For More Information Contact:
Teresa Skinner
PO Box 26632
Prescott Valley, AZ 86312
www.teresaskinnercom
jawa-art@as.net

Download the King Nebuchadnezzar song at www.teresaskinner.com

www.ingramcontent.com/pod-product-compliance
Lightning Source LLC
Chambersburg PA
CBHW041749290426

44112CB00004B/55